Trade Finance

Comptroller's Handbook

November 1998

A

Assets

Trade Finance

Table of Contents

Background

This booklet contains background and procedural guidance for examiners who evaluate trade finance operations. It combines the previous Comptroller's Handbook sections on letters of credit and guarantees-issued. Banker's acceptances, another trade finance product, are the topic of a separate booklet that has not yet been published as of this booklet's printing.

The expansion of international trade that supported growth in incomes following World War II has been accompanied by dramatic transformations in the economies of the United States and other countries. U.S. exports as a percentage of the gross domestic product (GDP) has been steadily rising since World War II; in the 1990s it has averaged 11 percent. An increasing number of U.S. jobs are associated with exports.

Governments around the world are supporting cross-border trade by coordinating the rules that govern it. In 1993, the United States and 116 other nations concluded the Uruguay Round negotiations of the General Agreement on Tariffs and Trade (GATT), a major multilateral trade agreement. The GATT establishes free trade principles and expands worldwide trade by reducing tariffs and other trade barriers, including export subsidies and regulations. Also in 1993, the United States, Mexico, and Canada completed the North American Free Trade Agreement (NAFTA). By integrating 370 million consumers and an approximately $6.5 trillion economy, NAFTA created one of the world's largest trading markets. Several other significant regional trade blocs have developed recently – e.g., the European Union.

As international trade increases, so does the importance of trade finance. The success of a nation's export program depends on the availability of trade finance, which facilitates the transfer of commodities and manufactured goods between countries. Trade finance, an important business for U.S. banks, generates more than $1 billion in revenue annually. Banks can participate in trade financing by providing pre-export financing, helping in the collection process, confirming or issuing letters of credit, discounting drafts and acceptances, and offering fee-based services such as providing credit and country information on buyers. Although most trade financing is short-term, medium-term loans (one to five years) and long-term loans (more than five years) finance the import and export of capital goods such as machinery and equipment.

To promote exports, many countries, including the United States, offer various guarantee programs to help minimize the lender's risk in international transactions. The Export-Import Bank of the United States offers the most notable U.S. government guarantee programs.

Risks Associated With Trade Financing

For purposes of the OCC's discussion of risk, the OCC can be said to assess banking risk relative to its impact on capital and earnings. From a supervisory perspective, risk is the potential that events, expected or unanticipated, may have an adverse impact on the bank's capital or earnings. The OCC has defined nine categories of risk for bank supervision purposes. These risks are: credit, interest rate, liquidity, price, foreign currency translation, transaction, compliance, strategic, and reputation. These categories are not mutually exclusive; any product or service may expose the bank to multiple risks. For analysis and discussion purposes, however, the OCC identifies and assesses the risks separately.

The risks associated with trade financing are: credit, foreign currency translation, transaction, compliance, strategic, and reputation. These risks are discussed more fully in the following paragraphs.

Credit Risk

Credit risk is the current and prospective risk to earnings or capital arising from an obligor's failure to meet the terms of any contract with the bank or otherwise to perform as agreed. Credit risk is found in all activities in where success depends on counterparty, issuer, or borrower performance. It arises any time bank funds are extended, committed, invested, or otherwise exposed through actual or implied contractual agreements, whether reflected on or off the balance sheet.

In trade finance, many transactions are self-liquidating or supported by letters of credit and guarantees, and the examiner must review each transaction individually to properly identify and evaluate the sources of repayment.

Although trade finance has a low loss ratio historically, it is a very specialized area, and a bank that lacks the appropriate expertise may experience losses because of improper structuring, poor documentation, unfamiliarity with a country's business practices, or improper pricing. A bank should ensure that documents on shipments of goods are proper and thorough. Any bank engaging in trade finance should thoroughly analyze the risks. In issuing a letter of credit for a domestic importer, the bank must evaluate the importer's repayment capacity as it would that of any other type of borrower. In confirming or accepting as collateral a foreign bank's letter of credit, a U.S. bank must evaluate the risk that the foreign importer/bank may not be able to raise the dollars required to repay the transaction because of capital controls in the importing country.

The Interagency Country Exposure Review Committee (ICERC) reviews and evaluates trade finance credits for transfer risk. Upon reviewing the history and performance of these types of transactions, the ICERC usually concludes that trade finance credits granted by U.S. banks to entities in foreign countries have a low risk of default.

The low default risk is due, in part, to the importance that countries assign to maintaining access to trade credits. In a currency crisis, central banks may require all foreign currency inflows to be turned over to the central bank. The central bank would then prioritize foreign currency payments. Trade liabilities would be more likely to be designated for repayment than most other types of credits. For this reason, trade finance is viewed as having less transfer risk than other types of debt.

Foreign Currency Translation Risk

Foreign currency translation risk is the current and prospective risk to earnings or capital arising from the conversion of a bank's financial statements from one currency into another. It refers to the variability in accounting values for a bank's equity accounts that result from variations in exchange rates which are used in translating carrying values and income streams in foreign currencies to U.S. dollars. Market-making and position-taking in foreign currencies should be captured under price risk.

In a trade transaction, foreign currency translation risk arises from the exposure to fluctuations in exchange rates whenever payments involve foreign currencies. The level of risk depends on the currency involved in the transaction, whether the bank creates an open position, the size of any maturity gap, and settlement uncertainties.

A bank financing an exporter's operation by discounting foreign-currency-denominated drafts or acceptances encounters foreign currency translation risk because of the time lag between its discounting of the draft or acceptance and its collection from the foreign importer or bank. The U.S. bank will be exposed to foreign currency translation risk from the time it discounts the instrument and pays the local exporter the dollar equivalent of the draft or acceptance until it collects from the foreign counterpart in the foreign currency. If the foreign currency depreciates in relation to the dollar during the time it takes the bank to pay the exporter and to collect on the foreign instrument, the bank incurs a loss.

When the U.S. exporter is paid by the foreign importer with a dollar-denominated draft, exchange risk may arise from transfer problems. Transfer problems may occur when the foreign importer is located in a country that is having difficulties accumulating hard currency reserves. In those circumstances, the foreign importer may have the local currency to repay its debt but be unable to purchase the dollars because of central bank controls over the sale of hard currency. The payment instructions to the foreign importer's bank could allow payment to be received from the foreign importer in local currency with the stipulation that, when foreign exchange in U.S. dollars is allocated by the government authorities for the transaction, it should be remitted to the exporter's U.S. bank. Depending on the scarcity of foreign exchange in the foreign importer's nation, the wait may be longer than anticipated, exposing the U.S. bank to exchange risk if it discounted the draft.

Foreign currency translation risk is further discussed in the "Foreign Exchange" booklet of the Comptroller's Handbook.

Transaction Risk

Transaction risk is the current and prospective risk to earnings or capital arising from fraud, error, and the inability to deliver products or services, maintain a competitive position, and manage information. Risk is inherent in efforts to gain strategic advantage, and in the failure to keep pace with changes in the financial services marketplace. Transaction risk is evident in each product and service offered. Transaction risk encompasses: product development and delivery, transaction processing, systems development, computing systems, complexity of products and services, and the internal control environment.

Transaction risk is also referred to as operating or operational risk. This risk is particularly high in trade transactions because of the high level of documentation required in letter of credit operations. Many transactions evolve readily from letters of credit to sight drafts or acceptances or to notes and advances, collateralized by trust or warehouse receipts. Repayment often depends on the eventual sale of goods and the accuracy of documentation. Thus, the documents required to secure payment under the letter of credit should be properly handled.

Compliance Risk

Compliance risk is the current and prospective risk to earnings or capital arising from violations of, or nonconformance with, laws, rules, regulations, prescribed practices, internal policies and procedures, or ethical standards. Compliance risk also arises in situations where the laws or rules governing certain bank products or activities of the bank's clients may be ambiguous or untested. Compliance risk exposes the institution to fines, civil money penalties, payment of damages, and the voiding of contracts. Compliance risk can lead to a diminished reputation, reduced franchise value, limited business opportunities, reduced expansion potential, and an inability to enforce contracts.

Compliance risk can be overlooked because it often blends into transaction risk and operational processing. In trade transactions, failure to comply with domestic and international laws, such as the anti-boycott provisions of the Export Administration Act or regulations enforced by the Department of the Treasury, Office of Foreign Asset Control (see the "Bank Secrecy Act" booklet of the Comptroller's Handbook), may result in fines and prevent the bank from collecting on a transaction.

The bank must be aware of the laws of the country in which the counterpart to the domestic customer is located. The bank must ensure that collection and penalty procedures stipulated in the contract are enforceable in the foreign country. For this reason many banks rely on foreign correspondent bank relationships in the countries where they are active but lack branches.

Strategic Risk

Strategic risk is the current and prospective risk on earnings or capital arising from adverse business decisions, improper implementation of decisions, or lack of responsiveness to industry changes. This risk is a function of the compatibility of an organization's strategic goals, the business strategies developed to achieve those goals, the resources deployed against these goals, and the quality of implementation. The resources needed to carry out business strategies are both tangible and intangible. They include communication channels, operating systems, delivery networks, and managerial capacities and capabilities. The organization's internal characteristics must be evaluated against the impact of economic, technological, competitive, regulatory, and other environmental changes.

Strategic risk in trade financing arises when a bank does not know enough about the region in which it is doing business or the financing product it is using. A bank considering whether to finance trade must carefully develop its financing strategy.

Reputation Risk

Reputation risk is the current and prospective impact on earnings and capital arising from negative public opinion. This affects the institution's ability to establish new relationships or services or to continue servicing existing relationships. This risk may expose the institution to litigation, financial loss, or a decline in its customer base. Reputation risk exposure is present throughout the organization and includes the responsibility to exercise an abundance of caution in dealing with its customers and community.

Trade financing is an area where reputation and market perception is particularly important. Trade financing requires expedient processing of operations and significant attention to details of documents. A bank's failure to meet these requirements may result in financial losses to the bank and its customers, and may diminish its business opportunities in the trade financing community. To regain its foothold, the bank may have to lower prices on its products and fund expensive advertising/public relations efforts.

Risk Management

In reviewing risk, examiners should determine that a bank has adequate safeguards in place to identify, measure, monitor, and control risks inherent in the trade finance area. Such safeguards include policies, procedures, internal controls, and management information systems governing trade finance activities. The importance of strong internal controls in this area cannot be overemphasized. There is a growing incidence of counterfeit letters of credit, totaling millions of dollars. Often, these counterfeit instruments are not identified in a timely manner. A significant amount of funds can be released before the schemes are detected. Bankers should closely monitor every detail of a letter of credit transaction.

Examiners should also assess the capabilities of the trade finance staff and the adequacy of their training. A bank's trade finance policy should identify the target market, prospective customers, and desirable countries, and it should set country limits and minimum standards for documentation. The bank's trade credit administration system should be documented in a complete and concise manner and should include, when appropriate, narrative descriptions, flowcharts, copies of forms, and other pertinent information. Adequate documentation is the principal means available to reduce or eliminate risks inherent in international trade. Therefore, operating policies and procedures should address the documentation requirements for each transaction, and internal controls should be established to ensure adequate reviews. A well-organized and efficient backroom operation is essential because of the amount of documentation involved.

There is always the risk that a shipment will be damaged or destroyed, the wrong goods will be shipped, or the quality of goods (especially if the goods are agricultural) will be lower than stipulated. Insurance coverage is crucial to protect the buyer, the seller, and the issuing bank from loss. Banks should not issue commercial letters of credit without satisfactory insurance coverage.

Settlement of Trade Transactions

Structure

Trade finance transactions can be structured in a number of ways. The structure used in a specific transaction reflects how well the participants know each other, the countries involved, and the competition in the market. Sales can involve prepayments, shipments by open account, collections, and letters of credit. All of these structures are likely to be encountered in trade transactions with most countries. However, open account sales prevail in Europe, whereas letter of credit transactions are the norm in sales to emerging market countries.

The seller may require prepayment in the following circumstances: (1) the buyer has not been long established, (2) the buyer has a poor credit history, or (3) the product is in heavy demand and the seller does not have to accommodate a buyer's financing request in order to sell the merchandise. Prepayment eliminates all risks to the seller.

Open account (unsecured) shipments are made when the buyer has a strong credit history and is well-known to the seller. The buyer may also be able to demand open account sales when there are several sources from which to obtain the seller's product or when open account is the norm in the buyer's market. This option places all risks on the seller.

Letters of credit allow the issuing banks to substitute their creditworthiness for that of their customers. At a customer's request, the issuing bank pays stated sums of money to sellers of goods against stipulated documents transferring ownership of the goods.

Collections are of two types: clean (financial document alone) and documentary (commercial documents with or without a financial document). A financial document is a check or a draft; a commercial document is a bill of lading or other shipping document.

A clean collection involves dollar-denominated drafts and checks presented for collection to U.S. banks by their foreign correspondents. In a documentary collection, the exporter draws a draft or bill of exchange directly on the importer and presents this draft, with shipping documents attached, to the bank for collection.

The bank's role in a prepaid or open account transaction may be to transfer funds at the order of the buyer to the seller or to provide credit information on either party. In collection and letter of credit transactions, the bank takes a very active role in the exchange of documents between buyer and seller.

The documents are the means by which the banker participates in the trade transaction, either as agent for the seller or financier for the buyer. The bank may also extend credit to the seller in anticipation of the incoming payment.

Trade Financing Instruments

There are various trade financing instruments. This section reviews letters of credit and guarantees-issued. Bankers acceptances are discussed in a separate section of the Comptroller's Handbook.

Letters of Credit

A letter of credit, the most widely used trade finance instrument, is the simplest and most effective way for banks to finance export and import trade. The letter of credit is a formal letter issued for a bank's customer and authorizes an individual or company to draw drafts on the bank under certain conditions. It is an instrument through which a bank furnishes its credit in place of its customer's credit. The bank plays an intermediary role to help complete the transaction. A letter of credit does not prevent an importer from being taken in by an unscrupulous exporter, because the bank deals only in documents and does not inspect the goods themselves.

The Uniform Commercial Code and the Uniform Customs and Practices for Documentary Credits published by the United States Council of the International Chamber of Commerce set forth the covenants governing the issuance and negotiation of letters of credit. All letters of credit must be issued:

- In favor of a specific beneficiary,

- For a specific amount of money,

- In a form clearly stating how payment to the beneficiary is to be made and under what conditions, and

- With a specific expiration date.

Commercial Documentary Letter of Credit

There are two major types of letters of credit used to finance foreign transactions: the commercial documentary letter of credit and the standby letter of credit. The commercial documentary letter of credit is most commonly used to finance a commercial contract for the shipment of goods from seller to buyer. This versatile instrument may be applied to nearly every type of foreign transaction and provides for the prompt payment of money to the seller when shipment is made as specified under its terms. There are three parties to any type of letter of credit: the account party (or customer), the beneficiary, and the bank. Generally, a letter of credit also identifies a paying bank. The commercial letter of credit is addressed by a bank to a seller (beneficiary) on behalf of the bank's customer, a buyer of merchandise (account party). The letter authorizes the seller to draw drafts up to a stipulated amount under specified terms and undertakes to provide eventual payment for drafts drawn. The beneficiary will be paid when the terms of the letter of credit are met and the required documents are submitted to the paying bank.

In determining which type of commercial documentary letter of credit is suitable for a particular transaction, one should consider:

- The nature of the merchandise.

- The relationship between the exporter and importer.

- The financial standing and reputation of the buyer, the seller, and the issuing (opening) bank.

- How many times the underlying transaction is taking place.

- The financing needs of the exporter and importer.

- The availability and cost of financing in different countries.

Commercial documentary letters of credit are issued in either irrevocable or revocable form. An irrevocable letter of credit is a definite commitment by the issuing bank to pay, provided the beneficiary complies with the letter's terms and conditions. An irrevocable letter of credit cannot be changed unless all parties agree. Conversely, the issuing bank can cancel or amend a revocable letter of credit unless the beneficiary is notified. Not truly a bank credit in function, the revocable credit is a means by which the buyer and seller settle payments. Because a revocable credit can be canceled or changed without notice, the beneficiary should rely not on the credit but on the willingness and ability of the buyer to meet the terms of the underlying contract.

The letter of credit may be sent to the beneficiary directly by the issuing bank or through the issuing bank's correspondent located in the same place as the beneficiary. The correspondent may act as an "advising bank." The advising bank acts as an agent of the issuing bank in forwarding the letter to the beneficiary and makes no commitment on its part. The advising bank facilitates communications between the issuing bank and the beneficiary in the advising bank's community. However, unlike a bank that "confirms," the advising bank does not assume any liability if the issuing bank fails to perform. Advised letters of credit will bear a notation by the advising bank that it makes "no engagement," or words to that effect. An irrevocable advised letter of credit is, therefore, the undertaking to pay of the issuing bank rather than the advising bank.

Some beneficiaries (sellers), particularly those not familiar with the issuing bank, ask the buyer to have the irrevocable letter of credit issued in the buyer's country and "confirmed" by a bank in the seller's country. Confirmed letters of credit bear the confirming bank's declaration, "We undertake that all drafts drawn . . . will be honored by us," or a similar statement. Because the beneficiary of a confirmed credit has a definite commitment to pay from a bank in its country, it does not need to be concerned with the willingness or ability of the issuing bank to pay. A bank may play more than one role. For example, an advising bank may add its confirmation and be designated in the letter of credit as the paying bank.

Payment terms of a letter of credit generally vary from "sight" to 180 days, although other terms sometimes are used. The letter will specify on which bank drafts are to be drawn. If the draft is drawn at sight, the bank will make the payment upon presentation of the draft, provided the terms of the credit have been met. If the draft is to be drawn at maturity, the bank accepts the draft (by stamping "accepted" on its face) and holds it until it is payable. Alternatively, the seller can hold the draft, or the bank or the seller can sell or discount it. (For additional information, please refer to the Comptroller's Handbook on "Banker's Acceptances.")

Certain commercial letters of credit, such as a "back-to-back" credit (a letter of credit issued on the strength of another letter of credit involving a related transaction and nearly identical terms) and a "red clause" credit (also called a "packing credit"), contain additional elements of risk, and banks should exercise caution in negotiating them. Timing is critical for back-to-back letters of credit because the back-to-back arrangement increases the possibility that goods will be shipped after the letter of credit's expiration date. Deferred payment letters of credit, which become direct liabilities of a bank after presentation and receipt of the beneficiary's documents, involve greater potential risk because of the length of time the credit is outstanding.

Back-to-back letters of credit are appropriate when an agent is an intermediary between a manufacturer of goods exported and a foreign importer, does not have the funds to pay the manufacturer, and does not want the manufacturer to know the name of the importer (because the manufacturer may try to deal directly with the importer). The exporter takes the letter of credit issued by the importer's bank to his bank. The exporter's bank issues a letter of credit in favor of the manufacturer based on the terms of the original letter issued by the importer's bank. The letter of credit issued to the manufacturer does not carry the name of the importer. Generally, a bank issues a back-to-back letter of credit if it is the paying bank on the original letter of credit and is willing to accept the credit risk of both the exporter and the original issuing bank, as well as the transfer risk of the importing country.

In a red clause letter of credit (a clause on the instrument is printed in red ink), the issuing bank authorizes a negotiating bank to advance funds to an exporter prior to the shipment of goods and presentation of documents. The red clause enables the beneficiary/exporter to pay its suppliers using another party's funds.

In collection and letter of credit transactions, the bank takes an active role in the exchange of documents between buyer and seller. These documents are the means by which the banker participates in the trade transaction, either as agent for the seller or financier for the buyer. The bank may also extend credit to the seller in anticipation of the incoming payment.

Standby Letters of Credit

Standby letters of credit are also a common instrument in trade finance. Like other letters of credit, standby letters of credit involve a customer, a beneficiary, and a bank. A standby letter of credit guarantees payment to the beneficiary by the issuing bank in the event of default or nonperformance by the account party (the bank's customer). Although a standby letter of credit may arise from a commercial transaction, it is not linked directly to the shipment of goods from seller to buyer. For example, it may cover performance of a construction contract, serve as an assurance to a buyer that the seller will honor its obligations under warranties, or relate to the performance of a purely monetary obligation, e.g., when the credit is used to guarantee payment of commercial paper at maturity. A bank issuing standby letters of credit has a different role from one issuing commercial letters of credit.

Activities Commonly Backed by Standby Letters of Credit

Standby letters of credit can be used as:

- Credit enhancement facilities

  The bank guarantees payment of a company's paper and the rating of the bank replaces the company's rating. In such a situation, the standby letter of credit often acts as a backup of bond issues or commercial paper facilities. Credit enhancement is the most common role of standby letters of credit.

- Loan guarantees

  Standby letters of credit have been used on behalf of bank clients to enable them to borrow from private and institutional lenders at more favorable terms than they could obtain from their own bank. If the issuing bank has a strong credit rating in the bond or commercial paper market, the customer can gain access to that rating with its lower rate of interest through a standby letter of credit. The private lender relies on the bank's letter of credit, knowing that the lender may draw on the bank for repayment if the borrower does not directly repay the loan.

- Advance payment bonds

  Standby letters of credit, which are often used when the account party is paid part of the contract value in advance, ensure return of the advance payment if the goods or services are not provided.

- Performance bonds

  A standby letter of credit can be drawn on only if the account party does not comply with the terms of a contract or if there are defects in its goods and services. Engineering firms, contractors, equipment manufacturers, and exporters are often users. To effect payment, the beneficiary must present a draft to the issuing bank accompanied by a statement citing the nonperformance of the bank's customer under terms of an awarded contract. The issuing bank is obligated to pay the beneficiary and then seek reimbursement from the customer.

- Bid bonds

  A standby letter of credit can be used to ensure that the account party's bid for a contract is sincere and that the account party will enter into a contract that is awarded.

There are many differences between standby letters of credit and commercial documentary letters of credit. Commercial documentary letters of credit are generally short-term payment instruments for trade finance, while standby letters of credit are written for any purpose or maturity.

Under all letters of credit, the banker expects the customer to be financially able to meet its commitments. A banker's payment under a commercial credit for the customer's account is usually reimbursed immediately by the customer and does not become a loan. However, the bank makes payment on a standby letter of credit only when the customer has defaulted on its primary obligation and will probably be unable to reimburse the institution immediately.

A standby letter of credit transaction holds more potential risk for the issuing bank than does a commercial documentary letter of credit. Unless the transaction is fully secured, the issuer of a standby letter of credit retains nothing of value to protect it against loss, whereas a commercial documentary letter of credit provides the bank with title to the goods being shipped. For reporting purposes, standby letters of credit (like undisbursed commercial letters of credit) are shown as contingent liabilities on the issuer's balance sheet. Once a standby letter of credit is drawn upon, the amount drawn becomes a direct liability of the issuing bank.

The bank must ensure that standby letters of credit are segregated or made readily identifiable from other types of letters of credit or guarantees. Standby letters of credit should be aggregated with other direct lending when determining compliance with the legal lending limit. Like commercial letters of credit, standby letters of credit are covered under the Uniform Customs and Practices for Documentary Credits.

Documents

The success of a letter of credit transaction depends heavily on documentation, and a single transaction can require many different kinds of documents. Most letter of credit transactions involve a draft, an invoice, an insurance certificate, and a bill of lading; governments regulating the passage of goods across their borders may require inspection certificates, consular invoices, or certificates of origin; transactions can entail notes and advances collateralized by trust receipts or warehouse receipts; and transactions can culminate in sight drafts or acceptances. Because letter of credit transactions can be so complicated and can involve so many parties (not to mention areas of the bank), banks must ensure that their letters are accompanied by the proper documents, that those documents are accurate, and that all areas of the bank handle them properly.

Documentation is of four primary types: transfer, insurance, commercial, and other. Transfer documents are issued by a transportation company when moving the merchandise from the seller to the buyer. The bill of lading is the most common transfer document.

The bill of lading is a receipt given by the freight company to the shipper. A bill of lading serves as a document of title and specifies who is to receive the merchandise at the designated port (as specified by the exporter). It can be in nonnegotiable form (straight bill of lading) or in negotiable form (order bill of lading). In a straight bill of lading, the seller (exporter) consigns the goods directly to the buyer (importer). This type of bill is usually not desirable in a letter of credit transaction, because it allows the buyer to obtain possession of the merchandise without regard to any bank agreement for repayment. A straight bill of lading may be more suitable for prepaid or open account transactions.

With an order bill of lading the shipper can consign the goods to the bank, which retains title until the importer acknowledges liability to pay. This method is preferred in documentary or letter of credit transactions. The bank maintains control of the merchandise until the buyer completes all the required documentation. The bank then releases the bill of lading to the buyer, who presents it to the shipping company and gains possession of the merchandise.

Insurance documents, normally an insurance certificate, cover the merchandise being shipped against damage or loss. The terms of the merchandise contract may dictate that either the seller or the buyer obtain insurance. Open policies may cover all shipments and provide for certificates on specific shipments.

The commercial documents, principally the invoice, are the seller's description of the goods shipped and the means by which the buyer gains assurances that the goods shipped are the same as those ordered. Among the most important commercial documents are the invoice and the draft or bill of exchange. Through the invoice, the seller presents to the buyer a statement describing what has been sold, the price, and other pertinent details.

The draft supplements the invoice as the means by which the seller charges the buyer for the merchandise and demands payment from the buyer, the buyer's bank, or some other bank. Although a draft and a check are very similar, the writer of a draft demands payment from another party's account. In a letter of credit, the draft is drawn by the seller, usually on the issuing, confirming, or paying bank, for the amount of money due under the terms of the letter of credit. In a collection, this demand for payment is drawn on the buyer. The customary parties to a draft, which is a negotiable instrument, are the drawer (usually the exporter), the drawee (the importer or a bank), and the payee (usually the exporter), who is also the endorser. A draft can be "clean" (an order to pay) or "documentary" (with shipping documents attached).

A draft that is negotiable:

• Is signed by the maker or drawer,

• Contains an unconditional promise to pay a certain sum of money,

- Is payable on demand or at a definite time,

- Is payable to order or to bearer,

- Is two-name paper, and

- May be sold and ownership transferred by endorsement to the "holder in due course." The holder in due course has recourse to all previous endorsers if the primary obligor (drawee) does not pay. The seller (drawer) is the secondary obligor if the endorser does not pay. The secondary obligor has an unconditional obligation to pay if the primary obligor and the endorser do not, therefore the term "two-name paper."

Other documentation includes certain official documents that may be required by governments in order to regulate and control the passage of goods through their borders.

Document Discrepancies

Document discrepancies can range from minor typographical errors, which the bank may correct, to misstatements or incorrect documents. When a bank discovers such errors, especially material discrepancies, it should notify all parties and amend the documents. If the bank does not do so, it stands to lose protection and rights. Ultimately, it is the account party's right to decide whether to accept the documents with discrepancies or to delay or even cancel the transaction.

Bills of lading note most discrepancies. If the bill is "unclean" or "foul," notations on it will say that the merchandise was received in defective condition or that it is the wrong kind of bill. Unless specifically stated otherwise, all bills of lading tendered under credits must be "order" bills as opposed to "straight" bills. An order bill, which directs the carrier to deliver the goods to the order of a designated party, is a negotiable document of title granted to the addressee. A straight bill, which is always so described in its heading, declares a specific consignee without including the words "to the order of." It is not a title document and therefore is not sufficient security for the issuing bank. Normally, straight bills are used only when the buyer has made payment in advance; they are seldom used under documentary credits. The table on the following page highlights some of the common errors in the documentation of letters of credit.

Common Errors in Documentation of Letters of Credit

Bills of Lading

1. Unclean (when there are conditions which are not properly noted or reflected).
2. Ports different from those in the letter of credit terms.
3. Does not indicate whether freight is prepaid.
4. A later date of shipment than that allowed by terms of the letter of credit.
5. Description of merchandise is inconsistent with other documents.

Invoices

1. Invoice name and address do not agree with letter of credit.
2. Quantity does not agree with other supporting documents.
3. Unit price or extensions of unit price are incorrect.
4. Certification required by letter of credit terms is missing.
5. Excess shipment, short shipment, or partial shipment, which may be prohibited by letter's terms.
6. Adjustments on previous shipments or charges that are not allowed under the letter's terms are shown.
7. Sale's terms omitted or incorrect.

Insurance Documents

1. Coverage differs from that required by letter of credit terms.
2. Claims are payable in currency other than stipulated in letter of credit.
3. Policy does not cover transfer between shippers, although bills of lading show the transfer will take place.
4. Insurance certificate is presented instead of policy, when policy is required.
5. Merchandise description is inconsistent with other documents.

Drafts and Other Documents

1. Draft is drawn to purchaser instead of issuing bank.
2. Drawer's name does not correspond to name on invoice.
3. Tenor of draft differs from that of the letter of credit.
4. Credit amount is disproportionate to quantity invoiced.
5. Certificates of origin do not comply with importing country requirements.

Guarantees-Issued

Guarantees and sureties are not permissible activities for national banks, except when they are incidental or customary to the business of banking. For example, these activities would be permissible when the bank has a substantial interest in the performance of a transaction or when the bank has a segregated deposit sufficient in amount to cover its total potential liability. A national bank also may guarantee or endorse notes or other obligations sold by the bank for its own account.

Under certain circumstances, foreign branches of U.S. banks may exercise powers usually in the province of local banks (12 U.S.C. 604a). Those powers include guaranteeing a customer's debts or agreeing to make payment upon certain readily ascertainable events. Such events include, but are not limited to, certain nonpayments (of taxes, rentals, customs duties, and transportation costs) and the loss or nonconformance of shipping documents. To comply with 12 U.S.C. 604a, the guarantee or agreement must specify a maximum monetary liability. The same statute subjects liabilities outstanding to any one customer to the limits under 12 U.S.C. 84 (lending limits).

A common example of a guarantee subject to 12 U.S.C. 604a is a shipside (steamer) bond. Frequently, in an international sale of goods, the merchandise arrives at the importer's (buyer's) port before the arrival of correct and complete bills of lading. In such instances, it is customary for the importer (buyer) to obtain immediate possession of the goods by providing the shipping company with a bank guarantee, often called a shipside bond, which holds the shipping company blameless for damage resulting from release of the goods without proper or complete documents. Usually, the bank's guarantee relies on a counter-guarantee issued by the importer to the bank.

The provisions of 12 CFR 28.4(c) (foreign operations) permit a national bank to guarantee the deposits and liabilities of its Edge Act and agreement corporations and of its corporate instrumentalities in foreign countries.

Government Programs

Several U.S. government agencies offer guarantees to reduce risk in international trade financing. For a fee, the agencies protect banks from commercial and political risk. Although the programs differ in cost and scope of coverage, they are all designed to encourage commercial banks to participate in export financing. These government programs have gained significance because of the debt crisis in less-developed countries during the 1980s, which raised banks' concerns about transfer risk. When program requirements are met, the banks are able to carry out trade financing operations and book assets that might otherwise have been subject to examiner criticism/classification. Programs have varying conditions and requirements. The bank should maintain documentation in the file on program specifics. The requirements of each program should be reviewed by the examiner to determine the bank's compliance.

The Export-Import Bank of the United States (Eximbank) is the most widely known of the agencies. Eximbank was founded in 1934 to finance and facilitate exports from the United States to other countries. The agency encourages commercial financing of U.S. exports by guaranteeing repayment of loans made to foreign buyers of U.S. exports. In its lending, Eximbank must ensure that there is a reasonable assurance of repayment. Eximbank offers a variety of loan, guarantee, and insurance programs.

Eximbank offers a wide range of credit insurance policies covering the risk of nonpayment by foreign debtors. The policies, some designed specifically for financial institutions, cover certain percentages of commercial and political risks and interest repayment. Payment terms range up to seven years. Banks may obtain short-term policies (of up to 180 days) to cover the risks of:

- Participating in irrevocable letter of credit sales.

- Extending credit lines directly to foreign companies for the purchase of U.S. goods.

- Providing financing or guarantees on a U.S. firm's overseas receivables portfolio.

Eximbank's policy on bank letters of credit provides one-year blanket coverage insuring commercial banks against loss on their confirmations or negotiations of irrevocable letters of credit issued by foreign banks for U.S. exports.

Examiners are reminded that Eximbank discontinued its relationship with the Federal Credit Insurance Association (FCIA) in 1992. The FCIA is no longer backed by the full faith and credit of the United States government.

A list of Eximbank loan and guarantee programs appears in the table on the following page.

Eximbank Loan and Guarantee Programs

Program	Maximum Coverage	Repayment Period
Working capital guarantee To help eligible exporters obtain pre-export financing.	Covers up to 100% of the loan's principal and interest.	Usually up to 12 months.
Eximbank guarantee program Guarantees repayment of fixed or floating rate export loans from U.S. or foreign lenders to foreign buyers of U.S. exports.	Covers up to 100% of the guaranteed loan's principal and interest.	Usually from two to five years, depending on the contract value. Long-term repayment schedule runs up to 10 years.
Direct loan Provides competitive, fixed interest rate loans to help foreign buyers of U.S. exports. The proceeds from such loans are paid to U.S. suppliers.	Covers up to 85% of the contract price.	Usually from two to five years, depending on the contract value. Long-term repayment schedule runs up to 10 years.
Intermediary loan Provides a fixed interest rate loan to lenders that extend loans to buyers of U.S. exports.	Covers the outstanding balance of the lender's export loan, but no more than 85% of the contract price.	Varies from two to five years, depending on the contract value. Also, can provide a long-term repayment schedule not exceeding 10 years.

Other agencies or institutions that facilitate trade:

The Overseas Private Investment Corporation (OPIC) is a U.S. government agency that began operations in 1971. OPIC's mission is to promote economic growth in developing countries by encouraging U.S. private investment in those nations. It provides project financing, investment insurance, and a variety of investor services. OPIC's three principal programs cover financing of investments through direct loans, loan guarantees, and equity investments; insuring investment projects against political risks; and providing investor services such as country background information and advisory services. Investments approved by OPIC may be financed through commercial banks with a loan guarantee from OPIC, which protects banks and facilitates funding for private investment in developing countries. All of OPIC's insurance and guarantee obligations are backed by the full faith and credit of the U.S. government.

The Small Business Administration provides a revolving line of credit to fund the short-term needs of firms involved in exporting.

The Agency for International Development (AID) is an agency of the U.S. government responsible for foreign aid. It becomes involved in trade primarily by providing funds to emerging market countries and supporting development projects.

The Private Export Funding Corporation (PEFCO) is a private corporation owned by commercial banks, industrial corporations, and financial services companies. PEFCO mobilizes private capital to finance the sale of U.S. goods and services to foreign buyers. PEFCO funds itself by placing its obligations in public financial markets. PEFCO is not backed by the U.S. government. However, Eximbank supports PEFCO by guaranteeing the timely receipt of interest and principal on PEFCO's export loans, guaranteeing the payment of interest on PEFCO's secured debt, and making a line of credit available to PEFCO.

The Commodity Credit Corporation is an agency of the U.S. government that provides assistance in the production and marketing of U.S. agricultural commodities and related functions. The agency is also charged with the development of foreign markets and assists in the sale abroad of surplus agricultural commodities.

Relevant Legislation

Anti-Boycott Provisions of the Export Administration Act of 1979

The anti-boycott provisions of the Export Administration Act of 1979 (50 U.S.C. 240 et seq.) discourage and, in certain instances, prohibit U.S. banks from engaging in transactions related to unsanctioned foreign boycotts. The secretary of Commerce is authorized to enforce various provisions of the Export Administration Act, including issuing regulations to implement the anti-boycott provisions. Many states, including New York, Florida, and California, have implemented anti-boycott legislation.

The Department of Commerce regularly examines banks to determine whether they adhere to the anti-boycott prohibitions and has fined several banks for noncompliance. The Department of Commerce informs the OCC before examining national banks and, as much as possible, coordinates its on-site visits with the appropriate OCC supervisory office. The Department of Commerce also shares the results of its examinations with the OCC.

The anti-boycott provisions apply primarily to the issuance of international letters of credit that facilitate United States commerce, when the beneficiary is a United States citizen.

U.S. banks and their foreign branches, subsidiaries, and affiliates may not implement letters of credit containing prohibited boycott-related terms or conditions. Neither may branches, subsidiaries, and affiliates of foreign banks doing business in the United States. Common illegal boycott-related terms include:

- A requirement from a boycotting country for certification that the goods did not originate from a boycotted country. (A positive certificate of origin, however, is legal.)

- A requirement from the boycotting country for certification that the exporter/importer does not do business with a boycotted country.

- A requirement for certification that the supplier of the goods or a provider of services does not appear on the blacklist of a boycotting country.

- The words, "Do not negotiate with blacklisted banks," or a condition to that effect.

The act does not prohibit advising a beneficiary of the existence of a letter of credit or performing basic ministerial activities required to dispose of a letter of credit that contains prohibited boycott terms or conditions.

Reporting requirements for the act. Banks must report to the Department of Commerce letters of credit that they receive that include prohibited boycott terms or conditions. Oral requests to take action that would advance or support an unsanctioned foreign boycott must also be reported.

Criminal and civil penalties under the act. The law provides that whoever knowingly violates, conspires to violate, or attempts to violate the act or any regulation, order, or license issued under the act is punishable for each violation by a fine of not more than five times the value of the exports involved or $50,000, whichever is greater, imprisonment for not more than five years, or both. For certain willful violations, the fine is increased to $1 million for companies and $250,000 for individuals. Civil penalties may not exceed $10,000 for each violation, except when certain national security controls are involved, in which case the maximum is $100,000.

Examiner role. Examiners should review the adequacy of a bank's system for monitoring compliance with the act. Possible violations of the act should be discussed with district counsel and detailed in the report of examination (ROE) as appropriate. Information on sanctioned and unsanctioned boycotts may be obtained from the OCC's International Banking and Finance Division, Washington, D.C.

Export Trading Company Act of 1982

The Export Trading Company Act (ETCA) (12 U.S.C. 4001 et seq.), enacted in October 1982, encourages exports by facilitating the formation and operation of export trading companies (ETCs). This legislation encourages businesses to join together to offer export services by permitting certain banking institutions to own an interest in these exporting ventures and providing protection from antitrust laws.

An export trading company's principal business is to export American goods and services or help unrelated U.S. companies export their products overseas. ETCs can also periodically engage in importing and trade between third countries in order to promote U.S. exports. Foreign ownership of ETCs is permissible.

The general provisions of the ETCA, among other things, allow companies to pool resources through ETCs to market exports. The provisions authorize the Commerce Department to issue a certificate of review, which grants ETCs qualified immunity from criminal or civil actions under the antitrust laws.

The ETCA does not give banks (other than bankers' banks) authority to invest in ETCs. Congress attempted to reduce the risk posed by this breach in the traditional wall separating banking and commerce by allowing these investments to be made only through BHCs, Edge Act or agreement corporations that are subsidiaries of BHCs, and bankers' banks. The Federal Reserve Board, which has adopted regulations implementing the banking provisions of the ETCA, is the ETCs' supervisor.

The banking provisions allow bankers' banks and bank holding companies (BHCs) to own 100 percent of the stock of an ETC. Bankers' banks and BHCs also can invest up to 5 percent and loan up to 10 percent of their capital and surplus to ETCs. The Federal Reserve Board must be given 60 days prior notification of a BHC's intent to invest in an ETC, and may disapprove the investment during the 60-day period.

Credit transactions between a bank and its affiliated ETC are subject to the collateral requirements of 12 U.S.C. 371c. Covered transactions between a bank and an affiliated ETC in which a BHC has invested are subject to the collateral requirements of 12 U.S.C. 371c. An exception to these requirements is made when a bank issues a letter of credit or advances funds to an affiliated ETC solely to finance the purchase of goods for which the ETC has a buyer under a bona fide contract, and the bank has a security interest in the goods or in the proceeds from their sale at least equal in value to the letter of credit or advance. The Federal Reserve Board is authorized to waive the collateral requirement.

An ETC is prohibited from conducting certain activities. It may not engage in either agricultural production or manufacturing, except to repackage, reassemble, or extract byproducts to meet foreign requirements. An ETC owned by a BHC may not take positions in commodities, commodity contracts, securities, or foreign exchange except as is necessary to support its trade finance activity.

Other Legal Issues

Examiners should be aware of the laws that limit the amounts of certain kinds of letters of credit. Standby letters of credit and guarantees, which are defined as contractual commitments to advance funds, are subject to the limits of 12 U.S.C. 84 and must be combined with any other nonaccepted loans to the account party by the issuing bank (12 CFR 32.2 [f] [j]). Because commercial letters of credit are repaid in nearly simultaneous operations by exporter and importer and do not result in the bank granting a loan to the account party, they are not defined as contractual commitments to advance funds under regulations governing lending limits (12 CFR 32.2 [f] 2).

Commercial letters of credit issued on behalf of an affiliate are subject to 12 U.S.C. 371c when they are drawn upon and the bank is not reimbursed on or before the date of payment of the letter of credit.

Accounting Practices

All types of guarantees issued should be recorded as contingent liabilities on the books of the bank. Usually, the party for whom the guarantee was issued will reimburse the bank should it be required to pay under the guarantee; however, in certain situations some other designated party may reimburse the bank. This party may be designated in the guarantee agreement with the bank or even in the guarantee instrument itself. The bank may also be reimbursed from segregated-deposits-held or pledged collateral, or by a counter-guarantor.

Eximbank policies normally cover principal and interest. The interest, which is calculated based on the contract rate of the insured loan, will cover interest accrued until Eximbank settles the bank's claim. In the interim, loans that meet the nonaccrual definition must be reported as such in the call report (Schedule RC-N) until Eximbank settles the bank's claim.

Capital Requirements

For risk-based capital purposes, a 20 percent credit conversion factor is assigned to trade-related contingencies. Such contingencies are defined by 12 CFR 3 as short-term self-liquidating instruments used to finance the movement of goods and collateralized by the underlying shipment. A commercial letter of credit transaction is an example.

General Procedures

These procedures are intended to determine the adequacy of the bank's policies, procedures, and internal controls as they relate to trade finance. The extent of testing and procedures performed should be based upon the examiner's assessment of risk. This assessment should include consideration of work performed by other regulatory agencies, internal and external auditors and other internal compliance review units, formalized policies and procedures, and the effectiveness of internal controls and management information systems (MIS).

Objective: Determine the scope of the examination of trade finance and identify examination activities necessary to achieve stated objectives.

1. Review the following documents to identify any previous problems that require follow-up.

   - Supervisory strategy.
   - EIC's scope memorandum.
   - Previous Report of Examination and overall summary comments.
   - Working papers from the previous examination.
   - Audit reports and, if necessary, working papers.
   - Correspondence memorandum.

2. Review the UBPR, BERT, and other applicable reports. Identify any concerns, trends, or changes in trade finance.

3. Obtain the following from either the examiner performing the evaluation of loan portfolio management or the bank EIC:

   - Any useful information obtained from the review of minutes of the loan and discount committee or any similar committee.
   - Reports related to trade finance that have been furnished to the loan and discount committee or any similar committee, or the board of directors.
   - List of directors, executive officers, principal shareholders, and their interests.
   - A list of board and executive or senior management committees that supervise trade finance, including a list of members and meeting schedules. Also obtain copies of minutes documenting those meetings since the last examination.

4. Verify the completeness of requested information with the request list.

5. Determine, during early discussions with management, whether there have been:

    - Any significant changes in policies, practices, and personnel relating to trade balance activities, systems, loan approval or collection processes.
    - Material changes in products, volumes, and changes in market focus.
    - Levels and trends in delinquencies and losses for each loan type.
    - Any internal or external factors that could affect trade finance operations.

6. Review the bank's business and strategic plans and determine whether management's plans for the department are clear and reflect the current direction of the department.

7. Obtain the following, as needed, to perform the objectives and activities outlined in the examination scope memorandum:

    - The bank's current trade finance business and strategic plans.
    - The budget for trade finance at the beginning of the year, and budget revisions as of the examination date, along with the current profitability report.
    - An organization chart by function.
    - Copies of formal job descriptions for all principal trade finance positions.
    - Resumes detailing experience of principals in the department.
    - Copies of management compensation programs, including incentive plans.
    - Copies of key management reports used by department management.
    - Loan review reports covering trade finance since the last examination and copies of any management responses.
    - Descriptions of all codes and abbreviations used on computer-generated reports.
    - A summary listing of all trade finance products offered and a brief description of their characteristics, including pricing.
    - Each officer's current lending authority.
    - Current commission and fee structure.
    - Copies of marketing plans for the trade finance department overall and by product.
    - Copies of loan policies and procedures for all trade finance products.
    - A balance sheet and income and expense statement for the trade finance department as of the examination date and most recent year-end.

8. Obtain trade finance reports as needed on the following:

- Delinquencies.
- Participations purchased and sold since the preceding examination (including syndicate participations).
- Loan commitments and other contingent liabilities.
- Letters of credit issued (or confirmed) for major shareholders, officers, directors, and their related interests.
- Letters of credit issued (or confirmed) for employees, officers, and directors of other banks.
- Miscellaneous loan debit and credit suspense accounts.
- Shared National Credits.
- Interagency Country Exposure Review Committee credits.
- Trade finance transactions/loans considered problem assets by management.
- Specific guidelines in the lending policies, such as procedures for dealing with anti-boycott provisions of the Export Administration Act of 1979 and any state anti-boycott provisions, if applicable.
- Loans criticized during the previous examination.
- A listing of rebooked charged-off loans (arising from trade finance instruments).

9. Based on the performance of these steps and discussions with the bank EIC, determine the scope of this examination and its objectives.

Select steps necessary to meet objectives from among the following examination procedures. Seldom will every step be required.

Quantity of Risk

Conclusion: The quantity of risk is (low, moderate, high).

Objective: To determine the level of credit risk in trade finance, while evaluating the portfolio for collateral sufficiency and collectibility.

Underwriting and Testing

1. Assess the risk of new products implemented since the last examination and, to the extent possible, the risk of planned products.

2. Establish goals for testing the quantity of risk in the portfolio. Consider tests already performed by loan review and audit staff to avoid duplication for areas like:

   - Underwriting practices.
   - Product performance.
   - Management information systems.

3. Using the appropriate sampling technique, select customers for review. Transcribe file information which may include:

   - Customer's aggregate liability on letters of credit and guarantees-issued.

   - Detailed information on letters of credit and guarantees-issued which aggregate a customer/account party's total outstanding liability including:

) Undrawn amount.
) Date of issuance.
) Expiration date of the credit.
) Name of the beneficiary.
) Tenor of the drafts to be drawn.
) Purpose for the credit.
) Whether issued or confirmed.
) Whether revocable or irrevocable.
) Whether negotiable or nonnegotiable.
) Whether revolving.
) Whether cumulative or noncumulative.
) Whether transferable.

) Whether assignable.
) Whether there are amendments.
) Whether issued on behalf of domestic banks.
) Whether application (with official approval) is on file and in agreement with letter of credit terms.
) Whether bank's copy is initialed by the officer who signed the original letter of credit.

4. For loan commitments and other contingent liabilities of which the borrower has been made aware, analyze them if any current loan balance plus the commitment or other contingent liability exceeds the cutoff.

5. Determine compliance with policy including credit criteria, documentation, pricing, and terms.

6. Evaluate the credit risk of sampled borrowers by:

- Analyzing balance sheet and profit and loss items as reflected in current and preceding financial statements, and determining whether any favorable or adverse trends exist.

- Relating items or groups of items in the current financial statements to other items or groups of items set forth in the statements, and determining whether any favorable or adverse ratios exist.

- Reviewing components of the balance sheet as reflected in the current financial statements, and determining whether each item is reasonable in relation to the total financial structure.

- Reviewing supporting information for the major balance sheet items and the techniques used in consolidation, and determining the primary sources of repayment, and evaluating the adequacy of those sources.

- Reviewing compliance with provisions of trade finance agreements.

- Reviewing a digest of officers' memorandums, mercantile reports, credit hecks, and correspondence to determining the existence of any problems that might deter the contractual liquidation program.

- Relating any collateral values, including "margin" and "cash collateral" deposits, to outstanding trade finance instrument.

- Comparing fees charged to the bank's fee schedule(s), and determining whether terms are within established guidelines.

- Comparing the amount of the trade finance outstanding with the lending officer's authority.

- Analyzing any secondary support afforded by guarantors/counter-guarantors.

- Ascertaining compliance with the bank's established policies.

Participations Purchased/Sold

7. Test participation certificates and records, and determine whether the parties share in the risks and contractual payments on a pro-rata basis.

8. Determine whether the books and records of the bank properly reflect the bank's liability.

9. Investigate any participations sold immediately before the date of examination to determine whether any were sold to avoid examiner criticism.

Insider Borrowings

10. Review any circumstances that suggest preferential treatment for officers, directors, and insiders of the bank.

11. Review any circumstances that might indicate preferential treatment for officers and directors of other banks.

12. Prepare "Report of Borrowings of Officers of Other Banks," if appropriate.

Suspense Accounts

13. Determine liability to the bank on drafts paid under letters of credit and guarantees paid for which the bank has not been reimbursed by the customer.

14. Discuss with management any large or old items.

Shared National Credits

15. Compare the schedule of trade finance instruments included in the Uniform Review of Shared National Credits program to the sample

selection to determine which of the sample items are portions of shared national credits.

16. For each sample item so identified, transcribe appropriate information from the schedule to line sheets, and return the schedule. No further examination procedures are necessary for these items.

Interagency Country Exposure Review Committee Credits

17. Compare the schedule to the sample selection to determine which letters of credit are portions of Interagency Country Exposure Review Committee credits.

18. For each letter of credit so identified, transcribe appropriate information from the schedule to line sheets, and return the schedule. No further examination procedures are necessary in this area.

Previously Criticized Loans

19. For letters of credit criticized during the previous examination, determine disposition by transcribing:

- Current balance and payment status, or

- Date the trade finance instrument was drawn down (refinanced), paid, expired or canceled, and the source of repayment.

20. For rebooked charged-off loans arising from trade finance transactions, determine whether they:

- Meet the criteria and terms of the bank's lending policy for granting new loans.

- Are subject to classification. If they are, list loans for charge-off.

Letters of Credit

21. Review red clause letters of credit (packing credits) to determine whether:

- Clean advance or anticipatory drawing finance to the beneficiary (exporter or agent) is authorized under the letter of credit.

- The beneficiary will undertake to deliver, before the expiration date, the shipping documents called for in the letter of credit.

- The foreign bank makes advances to the beneficiary and is paid by drawing its own draft on the issuing (opening) bank, or the beneficiary is authorized to draw its draft on the issuing bank and the drafts received that are charged to the importer.

22. Review travelers' letters of credit (sometimes used in lieu of travelers' checks) to ensure that:

- They authorize the issuing bank's correspondent to negotiate drafts drawn by the beneficiary named in the credit up to a specified amount upon proper identification.

- The customer is furnished with a list of the issuing bank's correspondents abroad.

- They are prepaid in full.

23. Review back-to-back letters of credit to ensure that:

- The backing letter of credit is properly assigned as collateral to the bank issuing the original letter of credit.

- The terms of the original letter of credit are identical to those on the backing credit except that the beneficiary and account party are different; the amount of the original is not greater than that of the backing credit; the expiration date has been brought forward to ensure that the transaction will be completed before the backing letter of credit expires; and the beneficiary of the backing letter of credit is a regular customer of the bank issuing (opening) the second letter of credit.

24. When reviewing standby letters of credit, consider:

- Whether they represent undertakings to pay up to a specific amount upon presentation of drafts or documents before a specified date.

- Whether they represent an issuer's obligation to a beneficiary to repay money borrowed by, advanced to, or advanced for the account party; make payment for any indebtedness undertaken by the account party; or make payment because of the account party's default in the performance of an obligation, e.g., default on loans, performance of contracts, or actions relating to maritime liens.

25. When reviewing deferred payment letters of credit (trade-related), determine whether:

   • They call for the drawing of sight drafts, with the proviso that such drafts are not to be presented until a specified period after presentation and surrender of shipping documents to the bank.

   • The bank's liability for outstanding letters of credit calling for deferred payment is reflected as contingent liability until presentation of such documents.

   • The bank has received, approved, and acknowledged receipt of the documents, thereby becoming directly liable to pay the beneficiary at a determinable future date.

   • The payment will be made to the beneficiary by a certain date quarterly, semiannually, annually, etc. (If the bank has advanced money to the beneficiary against the deferred payment letter of credit, with its proceeds assigned as collateral to repay the advance, the transaction should be treated as a loan rather than a deferred payment letter of credit.)

26. Review clean deferred payment letters of credit to determine whether:

   • They call for future payment against simple receipt without documents evidencing an underlying trade transaction.

   • Are shown as direct liabilities on the bank's records when drafts are presented by the beneficiary and received by the bank.

27. Determine whether an authority to purchase:

   • Grants recourse to the drawer, does not do so, or does not do so but is confirmed by the negotiating bank.

   • Contains a "Far Eastern clause" for drafts drawn on the buyer. This clause obligates the buyer to pay interest at a stipulated rate covering the period between payment to the exporter and reimbursement from the importer.

28. Review U.S. Agency for International Development (AID) letters of credit to ensure that:

- The bank has an AID letter of commitment authorizing the transaction.

- The bank has checked to make sure that all documents, including those presented by the beneficiary, comply with the terms of both the letter of credit and the AID commitment.

- A letter of agreement between the bank and the foreign government gives the bank recourse should AID fail to reimburse the bank.

29. Determine that for Commodity Credit Corporation (CCC) letters of credit:

- The bank has a CCC letter of commitment authorizing the bank to issue letters of credit to beneficiaries supplying eligible commodities to foreign importers.

- At least 10 percent of an amount covered by a letter of credit in favor of the CCC is confirmed, i.e., guaranteed by a U.S. bank for commercial credit risk. Determine whether the total value of the credit is advised through a U.S. bank.

30. Review Export-Import Bank of the United States letters of credit by determining whether:

- The bank has an agency agreement stating that Eximbank has entered into a line of credit for a stipulated amount with a foreign borrower; that the bank has been designated to issue the letter(s) of credit; and that any payments made under an Eximbank-approved letter of credit will be reimbursed by Eximbank.

- The bank has checked to make sure that all documents, including those presented by the beneficiary, comply with the terms of both the letter of credit and the Eximbank agreement.

31. Review advised (notified) letters of credit to ensure that the bank merely advises the beneficiary and bears no responsibility. (These letters should not be examined unless the bank has communicated the letter of credit terms erroneously to the beneficiary, thereby posing a possible liability for the bank.)

32. Review other types of letters of credit to determine whether the International Bank for Reconstruction and Development (World Bank), the Inter-American Development Bank, or the Overseas Private

---

Investment Corporation reimburse the bank for issuing letters of credit on their behalf.

Objective: To determine the quality of earnings provided by the trade finance area.

Pricing/Profitability

1. Obtain a profitability report for the area and compare performance to budget. Also review bank product profitability and loan pricing models to determine proper income and expense allocations.

2. Using management reports and the UBPR, review the department's performance by analyzing:

- Profitability trends.
- Delinquency trends.
- Loss and recovery trends.

3. Discuss with management adverse trends and large or unusual differences from budget.

Objective: To determine compliance with applicable laws, rulings, and regulations for trade finance.

Letters of credit

1. Letters of credit — independent undertakings (12 CFR 7.1016) Determine that outstandings are true letter of credit transactions rather than guarantees by confirming that:

- The independent character of the undertaking is apparent from its terms.

- The undertaking is limited in amount.

- The bank's undertaking is limited in duration, permits the bank to terminate the undertaking either periodically or at will upon either notice or payment to the beneficiary, or entitles the bank to cash collateral from the account party on demand.

- The bank either is fully collateralized or has a post-honor right of reimbursement from its customer or another issuer of an independent undertaking. If the bank's undertaking is to purchase documents of title, confirm that the bank has first priority to realize on the documents if the bank is not otherwise to be reimbursed.

2. Lending limits on standby letters of credit (12 CFR 32.2 (d) (e))

- Review letters of credit to determine which are standby letters of credit subject to 12 U.S.C. 84 (lending limits).

- Identified standby letter of credit must represent an obligation to the beneficiary on the part of the issuing bank to repay money borrowed by, advanced to, or advanced for the account of the account party; to make payment on account of any indebtedness undertaken by the account party; or to make payment if the account party defaults in the performance of an obligation.

- Determine whether the credit of the account party under any standby letter of credit is analyzed just as thoroughly as that of an applicant for an ordinary loan.

- Combine standby letters of credit with any other of the issuing bank's nonaccepted loans to the account party for the purposes of applying 12 U.S.C. 84.

- Identify standby letters of credit subject to a nonrecourse participation agreement with another bank or banks where the limits of 12 U.S.C. 84 apply to the issuer and each participant.

- Determine which standby letters of credit are not subject to 12 U.S.C. 84 because, before or at the time of issuance, the issuing bank is paid an amount equal to the bank's maximum liability under the standby letter of credit; before or at the time of issuance, the issuing bank has set aside sufficient funds in a segregated deposit account clearly earmarked to cover the bank's maximum liability under the standby letter of credit; or the OCC has found that a particular standby letter of credit or class of standby letters of credit will not expose the issuer to as much loss as a loan to the account party.

3. General notes to financial statements: commitments and contingent liabilities (12 CFR 11.928 (d))

- Determine whether the bank provides a brief statement on contingent liabilities, including standby letters of credit, that are not reflected on the balance sheet.

4. Anti-boycott provisions for issuance of letters of credit (15 CFR 769.2)

   - Determine that the bank is not engaging in transactions related to unsanctioned foreign boycotts.

   - Determine that letter of credit instruments do not contain illegal boycott terms.

5. Reporting requirements for anti-boycott provisions (15 CFR 769.6)

   - Determine whether the bank reports any written or oral information about unsanctioned foreign boycotts.

6. Exceptions to prohibitions (15 CFR 769.3)

   - Determine whether the bank reports agreements to comply with permissible requirements of import documents, such as nonexclusionary certifications of origin, and import requirements denying entry to goods and services from nationals and residents of a certain nation.

Guarantees

7. National bank as guarantor or surety on indemnity bond (12 CFR 7.1017)

   Ascertain whether a bank that is lending its credit, binding itself as a surety to indemnify others, or otherwise guaranteeing has:

   - A substantial interest in the performance of the transaction involved, or

   - A segregated deposit sufficient to cover the bank's total potential liability.

8. Foreign operations (12 CFR 28.4(c))

   - Determine whether the bank guarantees the deposits and other liabilities of its Edge Act and agreement corporations and corporate instrumentalities in foreign countries.

9. Letters of credit (12 CFR 7.1016)

- Determine whether the bank's obligation is legally a letter of credit or merely a guarantee.

10. Regulations authorizing foreign banks to exercise the usual powers of local banks; restrictions on such exercise (12 U.S.C. 604a)

- Determine whether the guarantee covers transactions permissible under this statute.

- Ascertain that the guarantee or agreement specifies a maximum monetary liability and that outstandings to any one customer do not exceed 10 percent of capital and surplus, unless the bank is fully secured.

11. Tie-in provisions (12 U.S.C. 1972)

While reviewing the guarantee credit and collateral files (especially guarantee agreements), determine whether issuance of the guarantee is conditional upon:

- The customer obtaining an additional credit, property, or service from the bank or its holding company, other than a loan, discount, or trust service (or providing an additional property or service to the bank or its holding company, other than a discount or deposit).

- The customer refraining from obtaining a credit, property, or service from a competitor of the bank or its holding company (or a subsidiary of its holding company), other than a reasonable condition to ensure the soundness of the credit.

12. Records to be made and retained by financial institutions (31 CFR 103.33)

- Review the operating procedures and guarantee credit file documentation, and determine whether the bank retains records of each extension of credit greater than $10,000, specifying the name and address of the account party, the amount of the guarantee, the nature and purpose of the guarantee, and the date thereof.

13. For policies and procedures dealing with federal and state anti-boycott provisions, determine that the bank:

- Has not engaged in transactions related to unsanctioned foreign boycotts.

- Reports to the Department of Commerce letters of credit it has received that include prohibited boycott terms or conditions.

- Reports to the Department of Commerce oral requests to take any action that has the effect of advancing or supporting an unsanctioned foreign boycott.

- Has not been the subject of an anti-boycott examination by the Department of Commerce or state regulatory authorities.

Objective: To determine whether the bank's trade finance documents and records are accurate and, if not, how much risk the inaccuracy poses.

1. Test the addition of the trial balances and the reconciliation of the trial balances to the general ledger.

2. Using an appropriate sampling technique, select trade finance instruments (letters of credit and guarantees-issued) from the trial balance.

3. Prepare and mail confirmation forms to account parties of letters of credit issued (exclude confirmed letters of credit, which are covered below) and guarantees-issued. Ensure that:

   - All confirmation forms are completed in the name of the bank, on its letterhead, and returned to its auditing department with a code designed to direct such confirmations to the examiners.

   - Confirmation forms include account party's name, identification number of the trade finance instrument, amount, commission/fee charged, and a brief description of any collateral or counter-guarantee held.

   - Letter of credit participations serviced by other institutions are confirmed only with the servicing institution. Letter of credit participations serviced for other institutions should be confirmed with the buying (participating) institution and the account party.

   - Guarantees serviced by other institutions, whether whole guarantees or syndicate participations, are confirmed only with the servicing institution (or lead bank). Guarantees serviced for other institutions, whether whole guarantees or syndicate participations, should be confirmed with the buying institutions and the account party.

4. After a reasonable time, mail second requests to ensure that:

    •   Failures to reply, exceptions, and differences are resolved.

    •   The bank's confirmation forms for letters of credit agree with incoming tested cable and subsequent written follow-up instructions from the issuing bank.

    •   Guarantee-issued instruments are complete, and date, amount, and terms agree with the trial balance.

    •   Confirmation is requested by the holder if any guarantees-issued are not held at the bank.

5. Examine letters of credit and accompanying documentation for completeness by determining:

    •   Whether they are supported by the required application, which displays officer approval.
    •   Whether all the documents listed in the covering letter have been received, and the letter of credit relates to the draft and documents submitted. Check the letter of credit number on the draft.
    •   Whether the letter of credit has expired or been canceled.
    •   Whether the available balance of the letter of credit is sufficient to cover the draft amount.
    •   Whether the exporter is making partial shipments in contravention of a letter of that allows only one shipment to be made for the full amount.
    •   Whether the beneficiary of two letters of credit combines the shipment and presents only one set of documents.
    •   Whether the bill of lading is a straight or order instrument.
    •   Whether the bill of lading is endorsed to the bank.
    •   That the bill of lading is not "foul" or "on deck," unless specifically allowed. (A carrier receiving damaged boxes or merchandise in poor condition notes these defects on the bill of lading, which then becomes a "foul" bill. The notation limits the liability of the carrier to a subsequent damage claim. The bill of lading should not allow merchandise to be shipped "on deck" unless the letter of credit specifically authorizes it.)
    •   That the commercial invoice does not exceed the amount available under the letter of credit.

- Whether the weight list detailing each shipping container and its weight certificate stipulating the weight of the merchandise as a whole is signed and agrees with amounts shown on other documents.
- Whether there is a copy of the packing list for each copy of the merchandise invoice.
- Whether the insurance policy or certificate is properly endorsed and covers the specific risks enumerated in the letter of credit, whether the amounts are correct, and whether the description of the goods conforms to that on the letter of credit.
- Whether the inspection certificate attesting to the quality, quantity, and condition of the merchandise is the same on all other documents.
- Whether the information on the certificate of origin agrees with the requirements of the letter of credit.
- That any required consular invoices are present.

6. Review letters of credit for illegal boycott terms.

7. Check to see that the letter of credit issued appears to be genuine and that the required authorized signature of an approving officer is on each letter of credit form whether issued or confirmed.

8. Check to see that the signature on the guarantee is authorized and that the initials of the approving officer are on the guarantee instrument, as required.

9. Review customer ledgers to determine compliance with line authorizations and letter of credit agreement terms.

10. If the bank has to pay a beneficiary under its guarantee, review disbursement ledgers and authorizations to determine whether payment was made in accordance with the terms of the guarantee agreement.

11. Review the bank's procedures relating to collateral by:

- Comparing any collateral held with the description on the collateral register.
- Determining whether proper assignments, hypothecation agreements, etc., are on file.
- Testing the pricing of any negotiable collateral.
- Determining whether collateral margins are reasonable and in line with bank policy and legal requirements.

12. List all collateral and documentation discrepancies, and investigate.

13. Determine whether any collateral is held by an outside custodian or has been temporarily removed for any reason. Forward a confirmation request on any collateral held outside the bank.

14. Determine whether files contain documentation supporting counter-guarantees or letters of credit, when appropriate.

15. Review participation agreements for letters of credit and guarantees, excerpting, when necessary, such items as rate of service fee, interest rate, and remittance requirements. Determine compliance.

16. Review fees-collected accounts for guarantee instruments and the commission accounts relating to issuing, amending, confirming, and negotiating letters of credit by:

    • Reviewing and testing procedures for accounting for fees collected and commissions and the handling of adjustment.

    • Scanning fees collected and commissions for any unusual entries and following up on any unusual items by tracing them to initial and supporting records.

17. Make sure that the bank is submitting reports required by the anti-boycott provisions of the Export Administration Act of 1979 to the Department of Commerce.

Quality of Risk Management

Conclusion: The quality of risk management is (strong, satisfactory, weak).

Conclusion: The board (has/has not) established effective polices and standards governing trade finance operations.

Objective: To determine whether the board of directors has adopted policies for trade finance that are consistent with safe and sound banking practices and appropriate to the size of the bank and the nature and scope of its operations.

Policy and Strategic Planning

1. Determine whether management has clearly communicated trade finance strategic objectives and risk limits to the board of directors and whether the board has approved these goals. In coordination with the assessment of the overall strategic plan, do the following:

   - Determine whether the reports to senior management and the board of directors provide sufficient information to evaluate risk levels and trends.
   - Assess the format and clarity of planning reports. Are they easy to understand and interpret?
   - Assess the board's and senior management's ability to fulfill their oversight roles using the reports.
   - Evaluate the system used to test the accuracy of planning reports. Management's testing should be thorough and periodic.

2. Determine whether planning activities consider credit culture and loan policy issues and are linked to business plans and budgets. Assess the following:

   - The consistency between the stated or implied cultural philosophy and the objectives in the strategic plan.
   - The review process for budgets, business plans, and strategic plans to ensure that they are consistent and achievable.
   - How the bank evaluates a plan's implications for risk.

3. Verify that the board of directors and senior management routinely compare performance with planned performance. Evaluate the board's and senior management's review.

4. Evaluate the MIS used to make the foregoing comparison. Determine whether performance reports address the following subjects:

    •   Earnings and capital relative to risk measurements and objectives.
    •   Pricing objectives.
    •   Market share objectives.
    •   Credit quality goals.

5. In coordination with the overall evaluation of the strategic plan, evaluate the trade finance planning process for thoroughness and reasonableness. Do plans consider internal strengths and weaknesses, as well as external opportunities and threats?

6. Determine whether the trade finance planning process provides for periodic reassessments of strategic objectives.

7. Assess the process for making changes to the trade finance portfolio. Determine whether changes have been made, and analyze the changes to the plan.

8. Evaluate the bank's business, marketing, and compensation plans in the trade finance area to ensure that short-term goals and incentives do not promote behaviors that are inconsistent with strategic portfolio objectives and established risk tolerances. Determine whether management conducted a similar analysis.

9. Assess the loan policy to determine whether it provides appropriate guidance for the bank's lending activities. Consider:

    •   Approval process and authority levels.
    •   Delivery system/distribution channel.

10. Determine whether risk limits are well-defined and reasonable. Consider the way these limits are measured and the impact on the bank if the risk limit is reached. Determine whether capital and earnings at risk are used to define the risk limit.

11. Determine how compliance with risk limits is monitored and reported to senior management and the board of directors.

12. Determine whether the board of directors has approved the loan policy and whether the policy articulates the desired credit culture.

Processes

Conclusion: Processes and practices governing how the bank will pursue its trade finance lending objectives (are/are not) effective.

Objective: To determine whether processes, including internal controls, are adequate.

1. Assess the efficiency and effectiveness of the bank's trade finance operations, taking into consideration the size and complexity of operations and the types of loans extended. Consider also:

    *   How trade finance operations are managed, including how:
        -   The loan is processed after approval.
        -   Loan proceeds are disbursed.
        -   Collateral and documentation are managed.
        -   Various reports (delinquencies, extensions, renewals, and irregular payments) are prepared.
    *   How the collection process is managed.

2. Review the process employed to establish risk limits. Consider management's objectives in setting risk limits.

3. Evaluate management's process for periodically reviewing and revising policies and procedures. Consider:

    *   Whether the process effectively incorporates necessary and timely changes.
    *   What method is used to communicate policies and procedures to the staff.
    *   How the communication system is evaluated for effectiveness and timeliness. (Discuss the system with staff members.)

4. If applicable, determine credit administration's role in formulating policy, monitoring compliance with policy, and monitoring lending practices and portfolio quality.

5. Evaluate the system to ensure compliance with underwriting standards.

6. Evaluate management's process for ensuring that new loan quality is consistent with policy and the board's capacity and tolerance for risk.

Loan Records

7. Determine whether the bank has adequate processes to ensure that:

    - Loan records are produced or reviewed by persons who do not also issue official checks or drafts singly.
    - Loan records are produced or reviewed by persons who do not also handle cash.
    - Subsidiary records for trade finance instruments are reconciled each day to the appropriate general ledger accounts.
    - Reconciling items are investigated by persons who do not also handle cash.
    - Delinquencies arising from the nonpayment of trade finance instruments are prepared for and reviewed by management in a timely manner.
    - Inquiries regarding balances for trade finance instruments are received and investigated by persons who do not normally process documents, handle settlements, or post records.
    - Bookkeeping adjustments are checked and approved by an appropriate officer.
    - A daily record is maintained summarizing details of transactions involving trade finance instruments, e.g., issuance, cancellation, renewal, payments received, and commission and fees collected, and that the record supports general ledger account entries.
    - Frequent trade finance instrument records and liability ledger trial balances are prepared and reconciled monthly with control accounts by employees who do not process or record the trade finance instrument transactions.

Commissions and Fees

8. Determine whether the bank has adequate processes to ensure that:

    - Preparation and posting of records is carried out or reviewed by persons who do not also issue check singly, issue drafts singly, or handle cash.
    - Independent commission and fees collected are calculated and compared with initial commission records or adequately tested by persons who do not also issue checks singly, issue drafts singly, or handle cash.

Documentation

9. Determine whether the bank has adequate processes to ensure that:

- Terms, dates, weights, description of merchandise, etc., on invoices, shipping documents, delivery receipts, and bills of lading are scrutinized for differences from letter of credit instruments.
- Invoices, shipping documents, delivery receipts, and bills of lading are signed as required.
- All copies of letters of credit are initialed by the officer who signed the original letter of credit.
- All amendments to letters of credit are approved by an officer.
- The bank is not engaging in transactions related to unsanctioned foreign boycotts.
- The bank reports any written or oral information about unsanctioned foreign boycotts. Such information includes prohibited terms in letters of credit.
- The bank reports agreements to comply with permissible requirements of import documents, such as nonexclusionary certifications of origin, and import requirements denying entry to goods and services from national and residents of a certain nation.
- The bank takes appropriate measures to correct and follow up on any deficiencies disclosed by a Department of Commerce anti-boycott examination.

Collateral

10. Determine whether the bank has adequate processes to ensure that:

- Multicopy, prenumbered records are maintained that:
  - Describe in detail the collateral pledged.
  - Are typed or written in ink.
  - Are signed by the customer.
  - Document the issuance of receipts to customers covering each item of negotiable collateral deposited.
- Receipt and release of collateral to borrowers and entries in the collateral register are performed by different employees.
- Negotiable collateral is held under joint custody.
- All evidence of collateral for a single loan is maintained in a distinct file.
- Receipts are obtained and filed when collateral is released.
- Securities and commodities valued and margin requirements are reviewed at least monthly.

- When the support rests on the cash surrender value of insurance policies, a periodic accounting is received from the insurance company and maintained with the policy.
- Record of entries to the collateral vault is maintained.
- Stock powers are filed separately to bar negotiability and to defer abstraction of both the security and the negotiating instrument.
- Securities out for transfer, exchange, etc., are controlled by prenumbered, temporary vault-out tickets.
- Security agreements are filed.
- Collateral mortgages are properly recorded.
- Title searches and property appraisals are performed in connection with collateral mortgages.
- Insurance coverage (including a loss payee clause) is in effect on property covered by collateral mortgages.
- Coupon tickler cards are set up covering all coupon bonds held as collateral.
- Written instructions are on file covering the cutting of coupons.
- Coupon cards are under the control of persons other than those assigned to coupon cutting.
- Pledged deposit accounts are properly coded to prevent the unauthorized withdrawal of funds.
- Acknowledgments are received for pledged deposits held at other banks.
- An officer's approval is necessary before collateral can be released or substituted.

Letters of Credit

11. Determine whether the bank has adequate processes to ensure that:

- Deferred payment letters of credit are recorded as direct liabilities of the bank after it acknowledges receipt of the beneficiary's documents.
- Letters of credit are included in "Other Assets" and "Other Liabilities" in the call report.
- Standby letters of credit are segregated or readily distinguishable from other types of letters of credit or guarantees.

Other

12. Determine whether the bank has adequate processes to ensure that:

- All trade finance instruments are assigned consecutive numbers and, if liabilities, are recorded as such on the appropriate general ledger account and on individual customer (account party) liability ledgers.

- Record copies of outstanding letters of credit and unissued forms are safeguarded during banking hours and locked in the vault overnight.
- Advised letters of credit are recorded separately, as memoranda accounts, from letters of credit issued or confirmed by the bank.
- Letters of credit that were issued with reliance on a domestic bank, whether on behalf of, at the request of, or under an agency agreement with the domestic bank, are recorded as contingent liabilities under the name of the domestic bank.
- Any commission rebates are approved by an officer.
- The bank has an internal review system that:
  - Re-examines collateral items for negotiability and proper assignment.
  - Test-checks values assigned to collateral when the letter of credit is issued or confirmed and frequently thereafter.
  - Determines that customer payments of letters of credit issued are promptly posted.
  - Discovers all delinquencies arising from the nonpayment of instruments relating to letters of credit.
  - Determines compliance with federal and state anti-boycott provisions.
- Lending officers are frequently informed of maturing letters of credit and letter of credit lines.
- When appropriate, trade finance instruments are safeguarded during banking hours and locked in the vault overnight.

Personnel

Conclusion: Management (does/does not) have the skills and knowledge necessary to manage the risk inherent in trade finance.

Objective: To determine management's ability to conduct trade finance lending in a safe and sound manner.

1. Through discussions with management, ascertain its knowledge of current policies and procedures.

2. Review the organizational chart in conjunction with management resumes to assess the overall structure and managerial experience of personnel doing significant trade finance lending. If no chart is available, discuss structure and experience with department management.

3.	Review management-prepared staffing analyses for the trade finance lending area to determine staffing adequacy.

4.	Evaluate whether staffing levels are appropriate considering present and future plans.

5.	Using the results of carrying out the quantity and quality of risk procedures, assess the level of competency of significant personnel involved in the trade finance lending functions.

6.	Determine whether bank staff acquires and retains the appropriate skills. Assess established training programs.

Control Systems

Conclusion: The control systems used to measure performance, make decisions, and assess effectiveness of existing processes (are/are not) effective.

Objective: Determine the adequacy of control systems used to monitor trade finance lending activities.

1.	Evaluate the methods and information management uses to monitor loan portfolio quality.

2.	Evaluate the controls management uses to monitor new loan volume, and whether the quality of new loans is consistent with policy and the bank's capacity and tolerance for risks.

3.	Determine whether loan review or internal audit reviews loans for credit quality and whether they draw a conclusion about the quality of the underwriting, the strength of the portfolio, and the effectiveness of controls.

4.	Evaluate the effectiveness of the loan review system and/or audit function in identifying risk in trade finance lending. Consider:

	•	Scope and coverage of reviews.
	•	Frequency of reviews.
	•	Qualifications of loan review and audit personnel.
	•	Comprehensiveness and accuracy of findings.
	•	Adequacy and timeliness of follow-up.

5. Review loan review and audit reports, and management's responses to criticisms and determine whether management instituted adequate corrective actions to address audit recommendations.

6. Evaluate the adequacy of the monthly MIS package used by senior management to monitor the trade finance loan portfolio. Consider whether reports:

    -   Include adequate information on the quality and volume of new loans and the overall quality of the trade finance portfolio by type of product.
    -   Are used to monitor levels and trends in renewals, extensions, delinquencies, losses, and recoveries.
    -   Are generated on loans by loan officer to determine any negative trends.

7. Determine whether the MIS used in trade finance lending provides management with sufficient information to monitor the quality of credit underwriting.

8. Assess the adequacy of controls used to ensure that all necessary parties review changes to existing trade finance policies before their final adoption.

9. Determine whether control functions are independent. Consider:

    -   Reporting lines.
    -   Budget oversight.
    -   Performance evaluation.
    -   Compensation plans.
    -   Access to the board.

Conclusion Procedures

Objective: To communicate findings and initiate corrective action when policies, practices, procedures, objectives, or internal controls are deficient or when violations of law, rulings, or regulations occur.

1. Prepare a summary memorandum to the EIC or examiner assigned loan portfolio management detailing the results of the trade finance examination. Draft conclusions on:

    *   The quantity of risk.
    *   The quality of risk management.

2. Also address in the summary memorandum:
    *   The direction of risk in the portfolio.
    *   The extent to which risk management practices affect aggregate risk.
    *   Appropriateness of strategic and business plans.
    *   Adequacy and adherence to policies and underwriting standards.
    *   Adequacy of MIS.
    *   Compliance with applicable laws, rulings, and regulations.
    *   Adequacy of trade finance control functions.
    *   Recommended corrective action regarding deficient policies, procedures, practices, or other concerns.
    *   The trade finance department's prospects.
    *   Other matters of significance.

2. For any risk identified while performing the foregoing procedures, determine its impact on aggregate risk and the direction of risk. Examiners should refer to guidance provided under the OCC's risk assessment programs for large banks or community banks.

3. Discuss examination findings and conclusions with the EIC. If necessary, compose "Matters Requiring Board Attention" (MRBA). MRBAs should cover practices that:

    *   Deviate from sound fundamental principles and are likely to result in financial deterioration if not addressed.
    *   Result in substantive noncompliance with laws.

MRBAs should discuss:

- Causes of the problem.
- Consequences of inaction.
- Management's commitment to corrective action.
- The time frame and person(s) responsible for corrective action.

4. Discuss findings with management including conclusions regarding applicable risks. If necessary, obtain commitments for corrective action.

5. As appropriate, prepare a brief trade finance lending comment for inclusion in the report of examination.

6. Write a memorandum specifically stating what the OCC should do in the future to effectively supervise trade finance lending in this bank. Include supervisory objectives, time frames, staffing, and workdays required.

7. Update the electronic information system and any applicable report of examination schedules or tables.

8. Update the examination work papers in accordance with OCC guidance.

Laws

Commission or Gift for Procuring a Loan	18 U.S.C. 215
Export Administration Act of 1979, Anti-boycott Provisions of	50 U.S.C. 2401
Foreign Bank Powers	12 U.S.C. 604a
Legal Lending Limit	12 U.S.C. 84
Loans to Affiliates	12 U.S.C. 371C
Loans to Insiders	12 U.S.C. 375a, 375b
Political Contributions and Loans	2 U.S.C. 431 (8)(B) 2 U.S.C. 441b
Tie-In Provisions	50 U.S.C. 1972

Regulations

Bank as Guarantor	12 CFR 7.1017
Export Trading Company Act	15 CFR 4001
Financial Institution Records	31 CFR 103.33(a)
Foreign Bank Operations	12 CFR 28.4(c)
Legal Lending Limit	12 CFR 32
Letters of Credit	12 CFR 7.1016
Loans to Insiders	12 CFR 215
Minimum Capital Ratios	12 CFR 3